THE ILLUSTRATED COOKIE

WRITTEN AND ILLUSTRATED BY
PIET HALBERSTADT

MACMILLAN · USA

MACMILLAN
A Prentice Hall Macmillan Company
15 Columbus Circle
New York, NY 10023

Library of Congress Cataloging-in-Publication Data
Halberstadt, Piet
The Illustrated Cookie / written and illustrated by Piet Halberstadt.
p. cm.
Includes bibliographical references and index.
ISBN 0-02-547438-3
1. Cookies. I. Title.
TX772.H35   1994
641.8'654 — dc20
94-1211
CIP

Book Design by Piet Halberstadt

10 9 8 7 6 5 4 3 2 1

Manufactured in the United States of America

Dedicated

To Yayoi

Acknowledgements to: Lee, Carol, Julia & Ben Boltin, for their support over the years & this book; Hal & Olga, Hans & Erik for being great family above and beyond the call of duty; Kay Parmentier for her whole-hearted support for this project from the minute she saw it, Eric Weingartner of Altura Systems for keeping the computer and me from crashing, Dorothy Lagermann of La Cuisine & Doug Schneider of Ateco for their time providing knowledgeable information and helpful advice; Phil Pochoda, A.K.A "The Agent", advisor and friend, Olgie P., Charles N; for their support during this project; The bakers: Georgine Dickieson, Fumi Dougherty; Doris Tsuchitani; Yayoi T. Tester T. Mizuhara Wendy Bass, for artistic and moral support. Justin Schwartz, the editor.

I would like to acknowledge and thank all bakers past and present that are a part of this book. Some of these recipes like Georgine's Cookies for a Crowd are family legacies passed on from generation to generation. Written on scraps of paper or index cards and stuffed into recipe files these coveted, little family treasures have been passed on to me so that I may share them with you.
It is with this spirit that cookies are shared around the world - in peace, fellowship and goodwill.

C O N T E N T S

I N T R O D U C T I O N

O F ALL the pleasures in life, making and sharing homemade cookies are amoung the simplest and easiest to enjoy for both the baker and the recipient. This collection celebrates the multiple ways cookies are made and is an excuse to bake if you need one

Methods of forming and decorating cookies are as diverse as those who bake them and the countries they come from. This book is designed to give directions for forming, baking and decorating many different types of cookies. The stages of baking and decorating have been arranged in the order they are used and performed; starting with equipment and ingredients and moving onto different methods of shaping unbaked dough, to decorative toppings. A slight change or addition to a recipe makes variations simple and easy. The freedom to experiment and create your own variations, shapes and decorations is encouraged. The gallery presents projects that are combinations of methods and illustrates earlier displayed recipe possibilities, variations and tidbits. Flavor combinations and cookie shapes are as endless as the imagination, and this book has been put together to encourage it. The purpose of this book is to have as much fun making cookies as it is to eat and share them.

Piet Halberstadt, New York City 1994

EQUIPMENT&INGREDIENTS

E VERY kitchen should have basic equipment such as measuring spoons and cups, mixing bowls, spoons and beaters. Additional tools like industrial-strength mixers can take a lot of the work out of a recipe or like a pastry crimper that cuts a fancy edge can add a decorative touch that might be laborious to do by hand.

Before investing in new equipment consider the basics first and add to your inventory of speciality items as needed. This book contains examples and recipes for a variety of techniques involving many of the basic tools used in molding and decorating cookies. The only speciality tools needed for baking cookies are baking sheets and cooling racks.

Quality ingredients help insure the success of a recipe. Each element used should be as fresh as possible. Baking soda for example has an expiration date. It becomes stale and loses its power over time causing a recipe to fail, so that all the hard work and caring put into the baking is wasted. Before starting a recipe take an inventory of the ingredients and be sure there is enough on hand. The chart of equivalents later in this chapter is helpful with shopping lists. Ingredients and yields are listed to provide a guide to amounts required, and if an emergency arises chocolate equivalents can be subsituted using cocoa or unsweetened chocolate.

BASIC EQUIPMENT

COOKIE SHEETS, not jelly roll pans are used for baking cookies. The sides of the jelly-roll pans impede the air flow around the cookie and makes them bake unevenly. Insulated sheets help keep cookies from burning by evenly distributing the heat to the baking dough. Baking times in this book are based on using uncoated, insulated sheets. Coated, nonstick finishes must be carefully handled. The coating is very soft and easily scratched;use hard plastic spatulas when removing cookies and and do not scour with metal pads.

OVEN THERMOMETERS are an important part in establishing control of the baking process. If the dial indicates 350°F, but the real temperature is 300°F or 400°F the only way of knowing this is to take the time to make sure you have set the oven to cook properly. Many cookies are burned to a crisp because the oven settings are not correct.

Cooking times in recipes can only approximate baking time. Each oven has its own characteristics and a recipe can produce a variety of results in different ovens. If timings are taken during a test batch, the baking consistency can be insured with a small timer.

ELECTRIC MIXERS, food processors and hand-held beaters do pretty much the same job as a hand-held wooden spoon. Making cookies does not require any electrical utensils, but electric mixers are much easier work if large quantities of dough are involved. The standing mixers allow freedom for the baker to do something other than holding the beater in the bowl.

SPATULAS are made in different materials for a variety of uses: wood, metal, hard and soft rubber for mixing the dough and thin; flexible metal for removing cookies from the sheet, loading a cookie press or spreading icing; and plastic for scraping down the sides of the bowl or folding ingredients into whipped egg whites. The professional metal variety are very flexible and strong. They are very helpful removing bar cookies from pans or reluctant cookies from baking sheets. Small metal spatulas similar to artists' palette knives are perfect for mixing colors or spreading icing on cookies.

WIRE WHISKS are used to whip egg whites and sometimes to fold in ingredients rather than using a spatula. A good metal, wire whisk has a weighted flat bottomed handle that acts as a counterweight allowing it to stand up by itself.

SIFTERS lighten ingredients, remove lumps or distribute other ingredients evenly in the mixture. They can be as simple as a fine mesh strainer that is shaken by hand, a hand crank or a squeeze-type.

WIRE COOLING RACKS allow air to circulate around the baked items so they cool quickly and evenly.

Specialty items like zesters and strippers make fast work removing zest from citrus like lemons and oranges. Pizza cutters and pastry crimpers are wonderful tools. They're easy to handle, not expensive and great for cutting dough into squares, rectangles and free forms. The pizza cutter cuts a straight line and the pastry crimper a decorative edge. Pastry brushes or pastry feathers are used to apply egg glazes to raw dough before they are baked. They should only be used for applying glazes and carefully cleaned after each use.

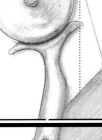

BASIC INGREDIENTS

FLOUR – unless specified use all-purpose, bleached or unbleached flour. The amounts listed in the ingredients list are unsifted. Cake flour and pastry flour have lower gluten contents than all-purpose. Cakes and other pastries utilize these qualities for lighter and softer results inappropriate for most cookies.

REFINED SUGAR is classified by the grain size. Always use "pure cane", the flavor is better. Regular granulated is the same as fine granulated or table sugar and is the most common. Unless specified the recipes in this book use this.

CASTOR or SUPERFINE has a finer grain and is commonly used in mixed drinks.

CONFECTIONERS' SUGAR, also referred to as powdered, icing and 10X, is a finely ground sugar with cornstarch added; usually used for frostings and icings, but also in some cookie recipes because of it's fine texture.

BROWN SUGAR is a soft sugar that has molasses crystals remaining from or added after the refining process. It is available in two flavor strengths, light and dark. I prefer the dark for the pronounced flavor. If substitutions for granulated sugar are made with brown sugar the flavor and texture will be affected.

CRYSTAL SUGAR has a large grain that is frequently colored and used as decoration.

SUGAR SUBSTITUTES replace the sweetness of

sugar but not the chemistry required for baking. Using substitutes will affect the taste and texture.

EGGS – use fresh, graded large or extra large. Refrigerated eggs keep fresh for 3 to 4 weeks.

BUTTER – Sweet, unsalted is used for baking. Almost all cookies use butter, not all use salt.

CREAM – use heavy (also called whipping) cream. This can be

stored, sealed in the refrigerator for 2 to 3 days.

SPICES should be stored air tight containers in dark places. Since this is not always the case, check the pungency before using. Some spices like cinnamon and allspice may be purchased ground or whole. If possible grind your own as needed. Small seeds like anise may need to be picked over to remove the dry leaf that remains with the seeds. Failure to do so may lead to cookies with a weedy texture.

FLAVORING EXTRACTS keep indefinitely if tightly sealed and stored in a cool, dark place. Pure extracts have the best flavor , and are also most expensive. Natural flavor-

ings have a color of their own and will tint the batter. If this color change is not to your liking choose a clear extract. Most extracts contain a high amount of alcohol (almost, if not more than bottled spirits) that burns off during baking. Store flavorings with alcohol with the same concern as for liquor.

ESSENCES are highly concentrated flavorings distilled from natural ingredients. Measure them by drops rather than teaspoons using a toothpick to dip into the bottle. Add drop by drop until the desired strength is reached. Exotic flavors available include lime, mandarin and grapefruit; even a cocoa essence to add to chocolate.

LIQUEURs are used for flavoring just like extracts. Many are available in small bottles called miniatures. These 50 milliliter (50ML) bottle holds 3 tablespoons plus 1 teaspoon of liquid. Here is a list of the

most popular liqueurs used in baking and an indication of their flavor.

Almond: Amaretto

Licorice (Anise): Anis and Sambuca

Orange: Cointreau, Curaçao, and Grand Marnier

Herb and spice: Drambuie, Bénédictine, and Chartreuse.

Coffee and cocoa: Kahúla

Banana: Banane

Blackcurrant: Cassis

Chocolate; Cacao

Coffee: Cafe

Mint; Mente

Raspberry; Framboise

Strawberry;

Fraise

HINTS, MEASUREMENTS & EQUIVALENTS

FIRST read the recipe completely. Many recipes fail simply because the cook didn't read and follow all the instructions. Inventory your equipment and make sure you have all the tools you will need in good, clean, working order. Prepare the working space and counter top to give enough clean area to function in. Check the larder against the ingredient list to avoid a rush trip to the market or worse, wasted effort and unsatisfactory results.

Other helpful hints:

• Color is the best indicator the cookies are done. The edges and bottoms will be just turning brown.

• An easy way to break up nuts for cookies is to place the amount of whole nuts you need into a plastic bag, tie up or close the end to prevent spilling and use a wooden rolling pin or wooden mallet to break the nuts into pieces.

• Cover a cookie sheet with parchment paper quickly by taking a wrapped stick of butter, uncover one end and draw a circle around the inside of the sheet and make an "X" through the center. The paper will stay in place and if an overhanging edge remains it is easily trimmed off with a sharp knife.

• Cream butter easily by allowing it to warm to room temperature before beating.

• Do not store cookies of different flavors together in containers or each may loose their distinct taste.

• Do not store crisp and soft cookies together. The crisp cookies will become soft.

• Soft cookies should be kept tightly covered. If they begin to dry out place a slice of apple in the container for a few days. This will replace some of the lost moisture. Remove the apple after cookie softens.

• Ingredients such as eggs, milk and cream incorporate better and easier when they are all at room temperature.

• Frosted cookies are best stored in containers between sheets of wax paper after they are thoroughly dry. This helps prevent them from sticking together.

• Measure

accurately and use measuring equipment. Liquid should be filled level with the rim, cups should be viewed horizontally to insure correct fill. Measure dry ingredients by over filling the cup then level off with the edge of a spatula or the back of a knife. Firmly pack brown sugar for proper fill and inspect for lumps. Discard the lumps if they are hard and cannot broken with fingers or spoon unless the sugar is going to be melted. These hard lumps do not break up in the mixing and usually leave an unsightly clump.

• To make a double boiler find a bowl that will sit in a pot or saucepan and overlap the rim. Pour water into the pan until it is about 1 inch deep.

• When baking do not mix different types and colors of baking sheets in the oven at the same time. Each has a slightly different baking time. If you do some may be scorched and others not done.

• Do not cool cookies too quickly or in a draft, they may crack.

Measurements & Equivalents:

Just in case you have run out of clean measuring devices and would like to know how much to buy for a recipe or need to make an unforeseen substitution here is some help.

3 teaspoons	1 tablespoon
4 tablespoons	¼ cup
16 tablespoons	1 cup
2 cups	1 pint

Flour
• 1 pound of flour equals about 4 cups

Sugar
• 1 pound of granulated sugar equals about 2 cups
• 1 pound of confectioners' sugar equals 3 ½ cups sifted
• 1 pound of brown sugar equals about 2 ¼ cups (firmly packed)

Butter
• 1 pound of butter (not whipped) equals 2 cups
• 1 pound container of butter has 4 - ¼ pound sticks
• 1 stick of butter equals 4 ounces,

8 tablespoons or ½ cup
• To get 2 ounces or 4 tablespoons halve the stick
• to get 1 ounce or 2 tablespoons halve the half
• To get 6 ounces. divide into 4 equal parts and remove 1 part
• 5 ⅓ tablespoons equal ⅓ cup

Chocolate
• 1 square of baking chocolate equals 1 ounce
• 1 square of baking chocolate equals 4 grated tablespoons
• 3 level tablespoons of cocoa plus 1 tablespoon oil or shortening equals 1 ounce (square) of unsweetened chocolate
• 1 ounce unsweetened chocolate plus 4 teaspoons granulated sugar equals 1 ⅔ ounce (squares) semisweet chocolate

Citrus
• 1 medium lemon yields about 3 tablespoons juice and 1 tablespoon grated rind
• 1 medium orange yields about ⅓ cup of juice and about 2 tablespoons of grated rind

BASIC DOUGH

COOKIE dough to the baker is like clay to the sculptor, but cookie dough is easier to work with and tastes better.

The recipes in this chapter have been assembled to cover popular, basic types of dough. Each one is a combination of simple ingredients that are easy to make as is or alter; a small addition of ground nuts, seeds, citrus rind, cocoa, or a change of flavoring extracts transforms one recipe into many.

The Basic Dough is a versatile enough to be flavored in many ways and to be dropped from a spoon, rolled flat and cut, shaped with a press or formed into a cylinder, chilled until firm and sliced with a knife. Later chapters explain these methods if you are not familiar with them.

The number of cookies each recipe produces has not been included because it changes with each method of shaping.

RICH BASIC DOUGH

1 cup (2 sticks) butter, softened

1 cup sugar

1 egg

2 $1/2$ cups flour, sifted

$1/2$ teaspoon salt

1 teaspoon vanilla

CREAM the butter with the sugar, until smooth. Mix in the egg and vanilla. Combine together the salt and the flour and sift into the mixture. Continue beating until well blended and smooth. Roll into a ball, wrap in plastic wrap or wax paper, flatten into a rectangle, seal and chill 3 to 4 hours or overnight. Preheat the oven to 375°F. Roll out the dough on a floured surface to $1/4$ inch thick. Cut into desired shapes and place 1 inch apart on ungreased cookie sheets. Bake until firm, 7 to 12 minutes, depending on size. Rotate cookie sheets back to front and top to bottom half way through baking. Let cool 5 minutes then transfer to wire racks to cool. Decorate as desired.

This recipe is easily doubled and can also be used as drop cookies, refrigerator cookies, used in a cookie press or rolled by hand in to teaspoon sized balls.

A few minor additions to the Basic Dough can easily make one recipe into many. For two versions from the same batch of dough simply separate about ½ the completed dough into different bowls. Select one of the suggested variations from the column on the right (flavorings are all for the Basic Dough recipe, divide as necessary) and thoroughly combine with the dough. Proceed as previously directed. This technique is very helpful if producing a lot of cookies and more than one flavor is desired. Or if you would like to experiment with different flavors or additions without jeopardizing a whole batch.

2 tablespoons ground walnuts, pine nuts, or almonds and ½ teaspoon vanilla

or

grated zest of 1 lemon and 1 teaspoon lemon juice

or

1 teaspoon grated orange zest and 1 teaspoon orange juice

or

2 tablespoons anise seed

or

replace the vanilla extract in the basic recipe with brandy, bourbon, rum or a liqueur.

BASIC BUTTER COOKIES

1/2 cup (1 stick) butter, softened

1/2 cup sugar

2 egg yolks

2 teaspoons vanilla

1 cup flour

CREAM the butter with the sugar until smooth. Beat in the egg yolks one at a time, add the vanilla, and blend thoroughly. Scrape down the side of the bowl, add the flour to the mixture, and beat until well combined. Roll into a ball, wrap in plastic wrap or wax paper, flatten into a rectangle, seal and chill 2 hours or overnight. Preheat the oven to 375°F at least 15 minutes before baking. Roll out the dough on a floured surface to 1/4 inch thick. Cut into desired shapes and place 1 inch apart on ungreased cookie sheets. Bake until the edges are light brown and centers are just firm, about 8 to 10 minutes. Rotate cookie sheets back to front and top to bottom half way through baking. Let cool 5 minutes, then transfer to wire racks to cool completely. Decorate as desired.

CREAM CHEESE ROLLED DOUGH

COMBINE the sugar, butter, cream cheese, egg and almond extract. Beat at low speed until the batter is light and fluffy, scraping down the sides of the bowl occasionally during mixing. Continue beating and add the flour, mixing until well blended. Roll into a ball, wrap in plastic wrap or wax paper, flatten into a rectangle, seal and chill 2 hours or until firm enough to roll out. Preheat the oven to 400°F. Roll out the dough on a floured surface to about ¼ inch thick. Cut into shapes and place on ungreased cookie sheets about 1 inch apart. Bake 7 to 10 minutes or until edges are lightly browned. Rotate cookie sheets back to front and top to bottom half way through baking. Let cool 3 minutes, then transfer to wire racks to cool completely. Decorate as desired.

3/4 cup sugar

1 cup (2 sticks) butter, softened

3 ounces cream cheese

1 egg, slightly beaten

1 teaspoon almond extract

3 cups flour

GINGERBREAD COOKIES

2 1/2 cups sifted flour

1/2 teaspoon salt

1/2 teaspoon ground cloves

1/2 teaspoon ground cinnamon

1/4 teaspoon ground mace

2 teaspoons ground ginger

1/2 cup (1 stick) butter, softened

1 cup granulated sugar

1/2 cup dark molasses

1/2 teaspoon baking soda

1/4 cup hot water

SIFT the flour, salt, cloves, cinnamon, mace, and ginger and set aside. Cream together butter, sugar and molasses until well blended. In a small bowl or cup dissolve the baking soda in the hot water. Alternate adding the flour mixture and soda-water to the sugar mixture, beating thoroughly. Wrap the dough in wax paper or plastic wrap, flatten into a rectangle, seal and chill 2 to 3 hours or overnight. Preheat the oven to 350°F. On a floured surface roll out the dough a little at a time, leaving the rest in the refrigerator until needed, to about 1/8-inch thick. Carefully cut out desired shapes. Transfer to ungreased cookie sheet with a spatula and place about 2 inches apart. Bake about 10 to 12 minutes or until lightly browned. Rotate cookie sheets back to front and top to bottom half way through baking. Cool 3 minutes, then transfer to wire racks to cool completely. Decorate as desired.

SCOTCH SHORTBREAD

SIFT the flour twice with the salt and set aside. Cream the butter until smooth. Gradually mix in the flour mixture and sugar a little at a time, beating after each addition. Mix quickly and beat only until blended. Roll into a ball, wrap in plastic wrap or wax paper, and flatten into a rectangle and chill 1 hour or until firm. Preheat the oven to 350°F. Place the dough between two new sheets of plastic wrap or wax paper and roll out to ¼ inch thick. Cut into desired shapes. Bake on an ungreased insulated cookie sheet for 5 minutes. Reduce the heat to 300°F and bake 20 to 30 minutes more. Rotate cookie sheets back to front and top to bottom half way through baking. Cookies should be light in color, not brown. Cool 5 minutes, then transfer to wire racks to cool completely. Decorate as desired.

2 cups flour

1 teaspoon salt

1 cup (2 sticks) butter, softened

1 cup confectioners' sugar

CHOCOLATE COOKIES

2 cups flour

1/8 teaspoon salt

1/2 teaspoon baking soda

1 tablespoon powdered
instant coffee

1 tablespoon hot water

1 1/4 cups sugar

3/4 cups (1 1/2 sticks)
butter, softened

1 egg, slightly beaten

1 cup plus 1 tablespoon cocoa,
preferably dutch process

MIX together the flour, salt and baking soda and set aside. Dissolve the coffee in the hot water and set aside. Cream the butter and sugar until light and well combined. Add the egg, dissolved coffee and cocoa, and beat until thoroughly blended. Sift in the flour mixture a little at a time, beating after each addition until smooth and all the ingredients are incorporated. At this point the batter may be pressed out onto ungreased cookie sheets; shaped into a roll and used as a refrigerator cookie or shaped into a ball, then flattened into a rectangle, sealed in plastic, and chilled then rolled out on a floured surface and cut into shapes.

Bake in a preheated 375°F oven on ungreased sheets for 10 to 12 minutes, until firm. Rotate cookie sheets back to front and top to bottom half way through baking. Cool 3 to 5 minutes, transfer to wire racks to cool completely. Decorate as desired.

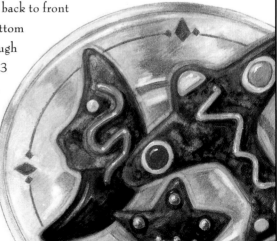

SUGAR COOKIES

MIX together the flour, baking powder and nutmeg set aside. Dissolve the baking soda in the hot water and set aside. Cream together the sugar, butter, salt, yolks and egg. Add the dissolved baking powder and water mixture and sour cream, and mix well. Gradually sift in the flour mixture and beat until well mixed. Roll into a ball, wrap in plastic wrap or wax paper, flatten into a rectangle, seal and chill 2 to 3 hours or overnight. Preheat the oven to 350°F. Rolled chilled dough on floured surface to $1/4$ inch thick. Cut into desired shapes and bake on ungreased cookie sheets 8 to 10 minutes, until the cookies are firm, but not yet brown. Rotate cookie sheets back to front and top to bottom half way through baking. Cool 3 minutes and transfer to wire racks to cool completely.
Decorate as desired.

2 cups flour

$1/2$ teaspoon baking powder

$1/2$ teaspoon nutmeg

$1/2$ teaspoon baking soda

1 tablespoon hot water

$3/4$ cup sugar

$1/2$ cup (1 stick) butter, softened

$1/4$ teaspoon salt

2 egg yolks

1 egg

$1/2$ cup sour cream

1 teaspoon vanilla

BUTTER DROP COOKIES

2 cups flour

1 teaspoon baking powder

¾ teaspoon salt

1 cup sugar

¾ cup (1 ½ sticks) butter, softened

¼ cup milk

1 ½ teaspoons vanilla

1 egg

PREHEAT the oven to 375°F. Combine the flour, baking powder and salt, mix well, and set aside. Cream the butter, add the sugar, milk, vanilla and egg, beat until well combined. Sift in the flour mixture, beat well. Roll the dough in teaspoon size balls with your hands and place 1 inch apart on baking sheets. Bake 9 to 12 minutes or until the edges are slightly browned. Rotate cookie sheets back to front and top to bottom half way through baking. Allow to cool on sheets 4 minutes, then transfer to wire racks to cool completely. Decorate as desired.

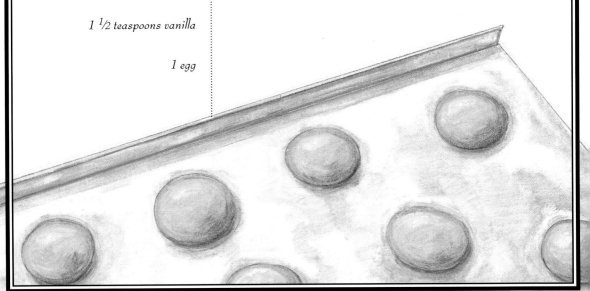

YAYOI'S BROWNIE / CHEESE CAKE BARS

BUTTER and flour 8–inch cake pan and set aside. Preheat the oven 325°F, adjust the oven rack to the middle of the oven. In a double boiler melt both chocolates and butter, whisk until smooth. Remove from the heat, stir in the salt, vanilla, and sugar, mix well then add the eggs one at a time stirring well after each addition. Add the flour and beat until the mixture is smooth and glossy. Add walnuts. Pour the mixture into a prepared pan, spread evenly. Prepare the Cheese cake mixture below.

2 ounces (2 squares)

unsweetened chocolate

5 ounces bitter sweet chocolate

1/2 cup unsweetened butter

1/2 teaspoon salt

1 teaspoon vanilla

1 cup sugar

2 eggs

1/4 cup flour

1 1/2 cups walnuts

CHEESE CAKE

IN A large mixing bowl, beat together the cream cheese, vanilla and sugar. Slowly add sour cream and lemon rind. Add eggs, beating until well incorporated. Pour over the brownie mixture. Bake about 1 1/2 hours. Cool in the oven at least 2 hours or over night. Chill before serving.

8 ounces cream cheese

1 teaspoon vanilla

1/2 cup sugar

1 cup sour cream

1 teaspoon grated lemon rind

2 eggs slightly beaten

CUTTING THE SHAPES

AFTER dough is rolled it needs to be cut. Simple straight cuts with a knife or pizza cutter, or crimped edges with a sharp pastry wheel are the most basic of all, but cookie cutters make fancier shapes.

Cuts should be made as clean and sharp as possible. Inspect cookie cutters before using to insure cutting edges are straight and clean. A long, thin bladed spatula slipped under a reluctant cookie will help loosen it from the cutting board and move it to the baking sheet.

The choice of cookie cutters designs has grown in recent years providing a huge selection to choose from. Imports from Europe include copper cats and hearts and new selections in tinplate include alligators and cactus while plastics provide familiar cartoon characters.

If a specific shape is not made, cut out your own with a stencil. This adaptable technique is used for special projects in the gallery for awards, clouds and thunder bolts starting on page 76.

COOKIE CUTTERS

THE first mental image of a cookie cutter that comes to mind is probably tinplate. Once produced by local craftsmen in tin these utensils have achieved folk art status. If your grandmother gave you one don't put it in the next garage sale, collectors and dealers are buying them and the prices have risen over the past few years. Cartoon characters like Donald were produced later on as early promotion pieces. New characters have their images now molded in plastic. Now you can decorate Big Bird and cookie monsters can eat Cookie Monsters. They carry on a tradition of marketing goodwill utilizing one of our most favorite and familiar foods.

Domestic manufacturers are still producing tinplate cutters in traditional shapes and have expanded their lines to include a wide variety of speciality figures and holiday shapes. There are baseball bats, dog bones, alligators, dinosaurs, ducks, hammers, and traditional shapes like crescents, gingerbreadmen and women; sets of different sized stars, hearts, plain and scalloped round cutters.

The renewed interest in baking has encouraged more products to be imported from overseas. Heavy-duty cutters with handles in tinplate and the more expensive copper are becoming accessible in a few speciality bakeware shops and through mail order.

Craftsmen are returning to tinshops to turn out hand made and custom cutters.

Tinplate cutters must be carefully washed to avoid damaging the metal surface. Avoid scrubbing with any abrasive cleansers and dry thoroughly to avoid rust. Some powdered dishwasher soaps discolor the metal.

Plastic cutters are now becoming more familiar to bakers. They are even sold in supermarkets. The cutting edge is not as sharp as tinplate. The cute shapes are popular with people cooking with children and handles on some cutters make them very easy for little hands to hold on to.

Additional store-bought cutters are small metal cutters are made for cutting everything from vegetables to aspics and are produced all over the world. Traditional Japanese cutters are used for cutting small, simple shapes and readily available in many Oriental food stores The Chinese manufacture intricate cutters in many shapes including dragons for use in their elaborate presentations. They are very beautiful and very expensive. Some are too intricate for cookie dough.

BEFORE you go running out to buy a simple cookie cutter look around the house. In these days of consumerism some people forget that before cookie cutters were so readily available and inexpensive, glasses, cups and saucers were flipped upside down and used to cut the dough or as a cutting guide.

A nice selection of round cutters are available by utilizing different size empty cans. Remove both ends of the can to allow air to escape easily as the dough is being cut and press down any sharpe edges left. The dull ends make them perfect for small children to use. Bottle caps and lids extend the selection even more. Use those like mayonnaise and soda bottles that have thin, straight sided edges to allow the dough to be cut with a clean, sharp edge. Inverted metal pastry tips cut fine small openings. If the dough gets stuck in the tip use a chopstick, the blunt end of a wooden skewer or toothpick to gently push the dough out. Saucers, square or round with or without fancy, scalloped edges can be flipped down and the shape cut with a knife.

STENCILS

IF YOU can't find a cookie cutter you like or would like to make something special all your own this technique is a useful addition to the baker's bag of tricks. Before starting consider the size and the shape of the stencil, remember that each cookie is going to be cut out by hand on a cutting area then transported to the baking sheet. The more complicated the shape, the longer and more difficult it will be to cut and moving it to the baking sheet could be difficult or impossible to manage. It can take hours to produce large quantities of large complicated cookies. Simple outlines are the most successful. Avoid cutting large holes out of the basic shape, or leaving narrow areas of dough, the cookie will become difficult to handle and may not bake evenly. A good shape could be anything from a tracing of a child's

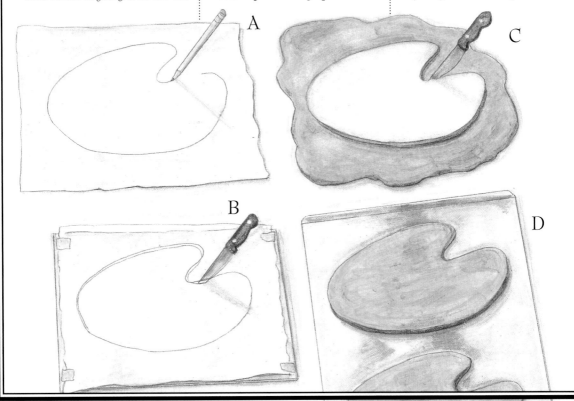

A

B

C

D

hand to abstract shapes that don't represent anything at all.

To make your own stencil cutout you will need: a clean piece of light bond, tracing or wax paper; paper, card stock or railroad board that is light enough to cut, but stiff enough to use again and again (a manila folder is a good example); a pencil and if you wish, a simple drawing or photograph to trace. Lay a piece of wax paper or tracing paper over the drawing and trace or draw a very simple outline (A). Again, remember that that you will be cutting out multiple copies in cookie dough using this pattern. After you have the outline of the image place the card stock to be used as the stencil on a flat cutting surface and tape the tracing to it. With a very sharp knife or a razor blade slowly and carefully cut through both pieces to produce a smooth outline (B). Apply pressure with your fingertips near, but not too close to the area you're cutting to keep the tracing flat on the card

stock being cut. Carefully remove the tracing sheet and inspect the stencil to make sure it is cut through all around the shape. If necessary carefully recut those areas still attached. The edge of the stencil should be smooth and neat. I prefer to use the inside piece because you can see the dough surrounding it, but you may use either.

After the dough is rolled out position the stencil on the dough and with one hand hold the stencil in place and cut with the other (C). Carefully transfer the cut out shape to the cookie sheet with a spatula (D). The baking time of the recipe used must be adjusted to the size of the cookie stencil. Test bake one cookie to establish the cooking time required for the remaining and if required lower the oven temperature.

To make a jig-saw puzzle stencil for cookies take a sheet of paper, a little smaller than the size of a cookie sheet or about 16 inches by

12 inches. With a pencil roughly divide each side into 4 equal parts marking all sides of the paper. Draw a grid using a ruler or a straight edge by connecting the marks on the opposite sides. Loosely indicate the jig-saw pattern by notching sections with rounded shapes giving a general impression of a puzzle. The grid will keep the cookies approximately the same size to insure a more even baking time for all the cookies. Cut the drawing into individual pieces or tape the uncut drawing over stencil board of about the same size as the drawing. Cut out following the instructions above.

Fun and simple shapes for stencils that are easy to cut and decorate include; skyscrapers, pillows, lightbulbs, computer diskettes, balloons, apples, carrots, mushrooms, rainbows, potatoes. Instructions for the Cookie Palette used in the illustration and other examples of using stencils are in the Cookie Gallery starting on page 76.

PRESSING, MOLDING & PASTRY BAGS

ROLLED by hand into balls, forced through a press into flowers or molded into Holiday figures, cookie dough is formed in a variety of ways using different equipment.

Different tools require different types of dough. Madeleines are made with an almost pancake batter that is cast into its shape in a metal mold, springerle has a very stiff, dry consistency that will not lose the design once its formed by a wooden mold pressed into it and a cookie press uses a moderately fluffy texture to allow for easy passage through the disk's holes.

A cookie press is an easy tool to use that produces cookies in many designs and in a consistent size. One batch of dough forced through an assortment of disks gives a simple dough a lot of variety for not a lot of effort.

Electric cookie molds produce a variety of familiar shapes. including fortune cookies, and sugar cones used to hold ice cream. A simple recipe for pizzelles on page 44 uses an electric press designed for these wafer-thin cookies. The batter is poured into the hot mold, the top pressed down and the cookie molds into the shape. It can be rolled into a cone while still warm and filled or eaten plain. This is the electrified Italian version of the stovetop Gaufrettes from France or the Scandinavian Krumkakes.

BASIC REFRIGERATOR COOKIES

1 1/2 cups flour

1/4 teaspoon salt

1 teaspoon baking powder

3/4 cup sugar

1/2 cup (1 stick) butter, softened

1 egg, slightly beaten

1 teaspoon vanilla

1/2 teaspoon grated
lemon rind

ADD the salt and baking powder to the flour, and set aside. Combine the sugar and butter, and beat until light and creamy. Add the egg, vanilla, and lemon rind, and mix thoroughly. Gradually sift in the flour mixture and continue mixing until the ingredients are well blended. Shape the dough into 2-inch round or square rods in 12 inch lengths (longer lengths are not as easy to handle) on a sheet of wax paper or plastic wrap. Seal the dough securely and chill until firm or overnight. Preheat the oven to 400°F. Cut the chilled dough into 1/8-inch slices with a sharp knife and bake on an ungreased cookie sheet 8 to 10 minutes. Rotate cookie sheets back to front and top to bottom half way through baking. Allow to cool 2 minutes then transfer to wire racks to cool completely. Decorate as desired.

VARIATION: Add 1/4 cup grated bittersweet chocolate and 1/3 cup chopped walnuts to the mixture after the flour is thoroughly incorporated.

SUGAR MINT COOKIES

COMBINE the flour, baking powder, and salt, and set aside. Cream together the butter and sugar. Add the eggs and vanilla, and beat until blended. Gradually sift in the flour and beat the mixture until smooth. Divide the dough into half. Add the mint and coloring to one half, and beat until blended. Wrap each in plastic wrap or wax paper, flatten into a rectangle, seal and chill 1 hour or until firm. Preheat the oven to 350°F. Roll the dough into a rectangle $1/8$-inch thick. Place rolled dough on cookies sheets for support and refrigerate for $1/2$ hour or until just firm, but not stiff. Place the one rectangle on the other with the vanilla dough on the bottom. Starting with the short side carefully roll up into a cylinder. Refrigerate again if the dough has become soft. Slice the roll with a sharp knife into $1/8$ inch pieces. Place 2 inches apart on cookie sheet and bake 8 to 10 minutes. Rotate cookie sheets back to front and top to bottom half way through baking. Cool 5 minutes and transfer to wire racks to cool completely.

VARIATION: Cut the rolled out rectangles of dough into squares or rounds and bake. Ice together with Cream Cheese Icing (see recipe on page 54) two cookies into sandwiched layers. Decorate as desired.

4 cups flour

1 tablespoon baking powder

$1/2$ teaspoon salt

1 cup (2 sticks) butter, softened

2 eggs slightly beaten

2 teaspoons vanilla

$1/2$ teaspoon mint extract

$1/4$ teaspoon green food coloring (optional)

CHOCOLATE WAFERS

2 ounces (2 squares)
unsweetened chocolate

1 1/4 cups flour

1/2 teaspoon baking soda

1/8 teaspoon salt

5 tablespoons butter, softened

3/4 cup sugar

1 egg

1 teaspoon vanilla

2 tablespoons milk

MELT the chocolate in the top of a double boiler, and set aside to cool. Mix the flour, baking soda and salt, and set aside. Cream together the butter and sugar. Add the egg, vanilla and milk, beating to combine. Sift in the flour, scraping down the sides of the bowl occasionally to insure the ingredients are well combined. Gradually pour in the chocolate, and beat well. Shape the dough into 1 1/2-inch round or square rods in 12-inch lengths (longer lengths are not as easy to handle) on a sheet of wax paper or plastic wrap. Seal the dough securely and chill until firm or overnight. Preheat the oven to 350°F. Lightly butter the cookie sheets. With a sharp knife slice the dough into 1/8-inch thick cookies and bake 8 to 10 minutes. Rotate cookie sheets back to front and top to bottom half way through baking. Allow to cool for 3 to 5 minutes, then transfer to a wire rack to cool completely. Decorate as desired.

BUTTERSCOTCH REFRIGERATOR COOKIES

MIX together the flour, cream of tartar and baking soda, and set aside. Cream the butter and sugar until light and well blended. Add the egg and vanilla, and mix well. Sift in the flour mixture and combine thoroughly. Stir in the walnuts. Shape the dough into a cylinder, transfer onto a sheet of plastic wrap, seal and refrigerate 3 to 4 hours or overnight. Preheat the oven to 400°F. With a sharp knife cut the dough into $1/8$-inch slices. Place on ungreased cookie sheets and bake 6 to 8 minutes. Rotate cookie sheets back to front and top to bottom half way through baking. Cool 3 to 5 minutes then transfer to wire racks to cool completely. Decorate as desired.

2 cups flour

$1/2$ teaspoon cream of tartar

$1/2$ teaspoon baking soda

$1/2$ cup (1 stick) butter, softened

1 cup brown sugar, firmly packed

1 egg, slightly beaten

1 teaspoon vanilla

$3/4$ cup chopped walnuts

DORIS' NEVER FAIL BUTTER COOKIES

4 cups flour

1 teaspoon baking powder

3/4 cup (1 1/2 sticks)
butter, softened

1 cup sugar

1 egg lightly beaten

2 teaspoons vanilla extract
or lemon juice

PREHEAT the oven to 400°F. Combine the flour and baking powder, and set aside. Cream the butter and sugar until well combined. Add the egg and vanilla, and beat well. Sift in the flour mixture and beat well, scraping down the sides of the bowl occasionally to insure a smooth, even mixture. Partially fill the cookie press and form into desired shapes on ungreased cookie sheets. Bake for 7 to 10 minutes or until very lightly browned on the edges. Rotate cookie sheets back to front and top to bottom half way through baking. Cool 3 to 4 minutes on sheets then transfer to wire racks to cool completely. Decorate as desired.

My friend Doris recommended the Atlas biscuit maker. After trying numerous cookie presses, including the electric versions she prefers to use this one. So do we.

MADELEINES

PREHEAT the oven to 400°F. Butter and flour madeleine molds, set aside. Beat eggs and salt until light and fluffy, then gradually beat in the sugar blending well. Increase the beating speed to high and continue to beat until very thick and lemon colored, add Cointreau after about 3 to 4 minutes. Slowly sift the flour into the batter and gently fold in by hand. After the flour has been incorporated, fold in the lemon. Add the butter by tablespoons and quickly fold in. Fill the molds 3/4 full and bake 8 to 10 minutes or until golden. Remove from the molds immediately and transfer to cool on wire racks. Dust with confectioners' sugar.

CHOCOLATE VARIATION: add cocoa to melted butter, mix well then combine with the batter.

3 eggs at room temperature

$1/8$ teaspoon salt

1 cup sugar

1 tablespoon Cointreau

1 cup flour

2 teaspoon grated lemon rind

$5/8$ cup clarified butter

Variation

2 tablespoons cocoa

SPRINGERLE

4 cups flour

$^1/_4$ teaspoon salt

1 teaspoon baking powder

4 eggs slightly beaten

2 cups sugar

2 teaspoons grated
lemon rind

2 tablespoons anise seeds
or to taste

Confectioners' sugar

SIFT together the flour, salt, and baking powder, and set aside. In a large mixing bowl beat the eggs at high speed until thick and lemon colored. Reduce the mixing speed to medium and gradually add the sugar, scrape down the sides of the bowl with a scraper and beat well to insure a smooth batter. Continue beating until very thick, about 10 minutes. Add the lemon zest and gradually sift in the flour mixture. Mix until blended and smooth. If the mixer is straining use a wooden spoon.

Prepare the cookie sheets by lightly coating with butter and sprinkling with anise seeds. Divide the dough into thirds. Roll out into a rectangle on a lightly floured board or marble to about $^1/_2$ inch to $^1/_4$ inch thick. Sprinkle the springerle pin, cookie block or mold lightly with confectioner's sugar. Be careful not to over fill the inside of the designs with confectioners' and clog the mold. Press or roll firmly and evenly. The impression left should be clear and the thickness of the cookies even. Only pass over the dough once with the mold. If required gently flip over the dough and reroll. With a sharp knife cut along the imprinted lines to separate the cookies, transfer with a wide spatula to prepared cookies sheets. Let stand covered with a clean dishtowel overnight in a cool, dry place. Preheat the oven to 325°F. Bake about 15 minutes or until golden. Transfer to wire racks and cool completely. Store in airtight containers 2 to 3 weeks before serving to allow the cookies to "mellow".

Families pass these heirlooms from generation to generation. Antique wooden and metal molds are rarely seen and have become very expensive. If you are lucky enough to own one treat it well. Excessive moisture will ruin the molds and rolling pins. Do not allow them to soak in water or scour with harsh cleansers. Wash by hand after use. Wipe thoroughly and allow to dry completely before storing. Do not clean in a dishwasher.

Springerle molds, rolling pins and metal molds are relatively easy to locate. Speculatius molds are still being made and are available from a few mail oder firms specializing in cooking and bakeware. La Cuisine has an impressive selection of these hard to find wooden blocks. See the Sources directory in the back of the book for listings.

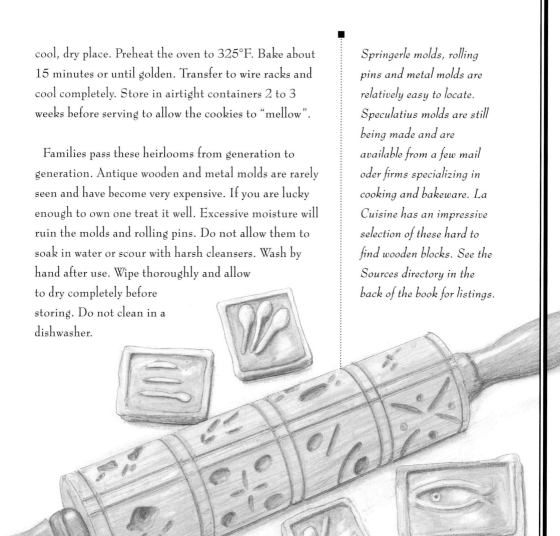

ELECTRIC COOKIE PRESS PIZZELLES

1 cup sugar

4 eggs slightly beaten

1/2 cup vegetable oil

1 tablespoon almond extract

2 teaspoons baking powder

1/4 teaspoon baking soda

1 3/4 cups flour

grated zest of 1 orange

GRADUALLY add the sugar to the eggs beating constantly until smooth. Add the oil, orange and almond extract, beat well. Add the baking powder and soda to the flour and sift into the batter, beat until smooth and well blended. Let the batter sit for 1 hour. Do not refrigerate. Preheat the closed press. Some presses have lights that indicate when heated. If not, drop a few drops of water on the grill they will dance when it ready to use. Before beginning to bake, have everything needed for this process arranged near by. These cookies cook in seconds not minutes and you can only produce one or two at a time. Have a clock with a second hand, wire racks for cooling, a round dowel, and a rolling pin or a metal cone for shaping near by and ready to go. Pour into the middle of the hot press 1 heaping teaspoon of batter, close the press and lock. Keep track of the time during the first cookie and cook the rest based on this test. Start the cooking time at about 15 seconds. Remove with a fork or thin spatula and transfer to wire racks to cool or form very quickly into cones or roll before they become too crisp.

TUILES

PREHEAT the oven to 425°F. Butter the cookie sheets and place away from the oven so the butter does not liquefy. Melt the butter and allow to cool. Combine the flour and salt and set aside. Mix together the egg, sugar and vanilla, and beat until fluffy. Gradually sift in the flour, and beat until well blended. Drop by measured teaspoons on the cookie sheet 4 to 6 inches apart. Bake one sheet at a time 3 to 5 minutes. Watch the cookies closely and remove when the edges are lightly browned. Allow to cool on the sheet 2 to 4 minutes. While the first sheet is cooling bake the next sheet. While the cookies are still warm, but cool enough to handle carefully lift them off the sheet with a spatula and form them around a thick wooden spoon handle or dowel. They will set quickly off the warm sheet. Place on wire racks to cool completely. Repeat with the next batch. Make sure the sheets are cool and well buttered before using for the next batch.

^{1}/4 cup (^{1}/2 stick) butter

^{1}/2 cup flour

1 pinch salt

1 egg, slightly beaten

^{3}/4 cup confectioners' sugar

1 teaspoon vanilla

EGG WHITES

THERE wouldn't be meringue cookies without stiffly beaten egg whites. The method of whipping them until smooth and firm is not difficult, but cautious steps need to be taken to insure a successful out come. Egg whites are easily contaminated by traces of oil or grease. To insure against this all the utensils used to whip the whites must be perfectly clean and dry. A preferred method of preparing equipment is to wash them in hot water, and allow to air-dry rather than dry with a cloth that may contaminate the utensils.

Egg whites beat better and easier at room temperature. A very small amount (less than a pinch) of salt added to the whites helps them liquefy. Cream of tartar may be used to keep the whipped egg white's firm and the color white. If using a copper bowl to whip egg whites, DO NOT USE cream of tartar. It causes a toxic reaction that turns the whites green and can be very dangerous.

Separating egg whites from the yolks is easy but must be done carefully. Crack the egg by hitting the edge of a bowl with a short, sharp movement. Hold one half of the egg in each hand and gently pour back and forth from one shell into the other. The white falls into the bowl below. Be careful not to break the yolk on a sharp point of the shell. Or gently break the egg and pour into a wide mouth soup spoon, held over a container. Carefully swirl the egg in the spoon as the white falls into the bowl below leaving the yolk in the spoon. Remove any shell that may have fallen into the bowl. Any yolk in the whites will not allow them to beat properly .

Bowls for beating egg whites in should be able to hold 15 times the unbeaten volume as correctly beaten whites expand to 10 to 12 times their original size.

TO BEAT: add salt to the whites and beat with an electric mixer or whisk at medium speed for a few seconds to break up the whites. Increase the speed to high. Continue beating until they firmly cling to the beaters and sides of the bowl. They should keep their shape when the beaters are lifted.

Tilt the bowl at a slight angle and beat with a large balloon whisk by hand using strong, circular strokes to lift the whites into the air. Start slowly to break up the whites, then increase the stroke as the whites thicken. Continue beating until they firmly cling to the whisk and sides of the bowl.

PASTRY BAGS

PASTRY BAGS come in different sizes and materials. The bags and metal tips used to pipe out cookies are larger than those used for piping out decorative frosting and icing. Prices vary dramatically from the expensive imported baker's bags to inexpensive light plastic. If planning to make hundreds of cookies on a daily basis buying an expensive bag is a good investment. The most popular and easiest to handle are plastic and plastic coated. They are inexpensive and light weight. Clean thoroughly with soap and water and allow to air dry completely before storing. Avoid canvas and nylon bags for cookies. The material is porous and allows liquid to seep through the sides.

Most bakers' have more than one set of pastry bags; one for recipes like buttercreams and another for batters like meringues that are easily ruined by grease.

A 14 or 16 inch bag with a plain, round, ⅜ inch tip is good for meringue cookies. Insert the tip in end of the bag, push it down and make sure it fits snugly and has no chance of sliding out. If a tip with pointed teeth is used make sure not to puncture the sides of the bag when inserted. Hold the tip end, twist the bag and push it inside the tip. This will prevent the contents from escaping while the bag is being filled. Fold back the top of the bag about half way down. This prevents the batter from getting on the outside of the bag. Spread the sides of the bag to form a funnel. Cradle the bag with one hand and spoon the batter into the bag, do not fill more than half way. An easier way to fill the bag is to place the tip end of the bag into a tall empty glass. Fold the cuff down around the outside of the glass and fill with a spatula. Unfold the bag, gather the top and twist to seal. Slide the neck through thumb and forefinger and push the batter toward the tip. Untwist the folds and pipe. Remember to keep your fingers clamped around the neck to prevent the batter from going in the wrong direction. The right hand holds the bag and controls the flow of the batter while the left hand guides the tip. When the desired amount of batter is on the cookie sheet end the movement with a sharp backward twist as the tip is lifted up. Remaining "tails" may be pushed down with a finger dipped in cold water.

Using a pastry bag for piping out cookies and decorating is very rewarding, but there is an art to working with pastry bags. Be patient and practice. The directions for Snakes on page 78 is a good exercise to practice with.

MERINGUE

6 egg whites

Pinch salt

1/4 teaspoon cream of tartar

1 cup superfine sugar

1 teaspoon vanilla or almond extract

PREHEAT the oven to 200°F. Make sure all the equipment used to beat the whites has been cleaned and is thoroughly dry. Start beating the whites and salt at medium speed to break up. After they begin to froth (about a minute), add the cream of tartar. Increase the speed to high and continue beating until they begin to hold soft peak, about 5 to 8 minutes. Continue beating and slowly add ¾ of the sugar. When the whites cling to the beaters and are shiny, stiff, almost dry and hold firm peaks, fold in by hand the remaining sugar and extract. Do not allow beaten whites to sit. Fit a large pastry bag with a large star tip and fill it half way. Pipe out on buttered and floured or parchment-lined cookie sheets. Bake for 2 hours with the oven cracked open to allow the moisture to escape. Turn off the oven and allow the cookies to dry overnight or transfer the cookies to wire racks and move to a warm, dry room.

Removing stubborn cookies from the parchment can be done by moistening the underside of the paper with a kitchen towel that has been run under cold water and wrung out.

OLGA'S MOTHER'S ALMOND MACAROONS

PREHEAT the oven to 325°F. Mix the confectioners' sugar and salt and set aside. Gradually work the almond paste with a wooden spoon or in a blender with the granulated sugar until smooth. Slowly add the confectioners' sugar and salt. Continue working the paste into a smooth mass. Add the egg whites slowly, fully incorporating each addition. Mix in the flour and beat until smooth. Pipe or press onto cookie sheets that have been covered with parchment. Bake about 30 minutes. Remove from the parchment with a metal spatula while still warm. Decorate with blanched almonds, pine nuts or small pieces of candied fruit.

1/2 cup confectioners' sugar

1/8 teaspoon salt

1/2 pound almond paste

1/2 cup granulated sugar

3 egg whites, slightly beaten

1/4 cup flour

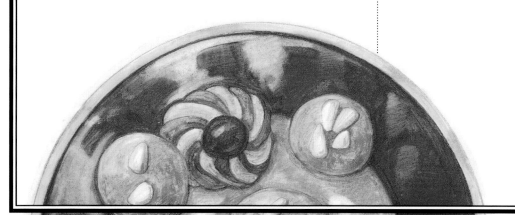

ICING & GLAZES

FROM a simple glaze of confectioners' sugar and water beaten together to elaborate, cooked icings (or "frostings", the words are interchangeable), these sugar coatings are more than decoration: they increase the taste, variety, richness and help keep cookies from drying out. Flavors and sweetness should compliment natural characteristics, not clash or overpower them. Using too much sugar is the most common and needless mistake. Too many delicately flavored and textured cookies are ruined by a covering of thick, sweet icing. No matter how beautiful a cookie looks or how much time is spent decorating it, the final judgement of a cookie's success or failure is its taste.

The range of flavors and sweeteners is not limited to bottles of extracts, fruit preserves, juices; syrups and liqueurs expand choices. Fresh fruits such as blueberries, blackberries, or tangerines have natural colors and flavors that can replace extracts and food coloring in icings. Fresh grated lemon or orange rind always gives more flavor and heightens the taste when added to extracts. Fresh ingredients, picked at the height of harvest celebrate each season in passing.

What would a Holiday Cookie be without colored icing? Intense colors from paste and powders or pastel shades from liquid add another dimension to the list of icing options.

BASIC SUGAR GLAZE

1 cup confectioners' sugar

*2 tablespoons milk,
half-and -half or cream*

Sift the confectioner's sugar into a mixing bowl and add the milk. Beat slowly at first to incorporate the ingredients, then increase the speed and beat until smooth and well combined.

VARIATIONS:
Add to the ingredients:
1 teaspoon lemon juice
        and 1 teaspoon grated lemon rind
                        or
                1 teaspoon orange juice
                    1 teaspoon grated orange rind
                or
            1 teaspoon of flavoring
        or
    1 teaspoon liquor: such as;
    brandy, rum, bourbon or liqueur

EASY ICING

MIX the sugar, salt, and vanilla; add the cream a few drops at a time beating after each addition, until the icing is smooth and holds a shape. Pipe out decorations colored as desired.

1 cup sifted
confectioners' sugar

1/4 teaspoon salt

1/2 teaspoon vanilla

1 tablespoon heavy cream

VANILLA ICING

MIX the ingredients in a small bowl at low speed, scraping down the sides of the bowl often to incorporate all the ingredients. Beat the mixture until smooth and fluffy. Separate quantities of icing to small cups or bowls and add color. Decorate as desired.

4 cups sifted
confectioners' sugar

1/2 cup (1 stick) butter, softened

3 to 4 tablespoons milk

2 teaspoons vanilla

CREAM CHEESE ICING

8 ounces cream cheese

1/2 teaspoon vanilla

1 tablespoon melted butter

2 1/4 cups sifted
confectioners' sugar

MIX the cream cheese, vanilla and melted butter. Sift in the confectioners' sugar and beat until smooth. Color as desired

MOCHA ICING

1 teaspoon powdered instant
espresso or coffee

1 teaspoon boiling water

2 tablespoons butter, softened

3/4 cup confectioners' sugar

water

IN A medium size bowl dissolve the instant coffee and water. Blend in the butter. Sift in the sugar beating continuously until smooth, a few drops of water may be added if necessary.

CHOCOLATE BUTTER ICING

MELT the chocolate in the top of a double boiler. Set aside to cool to room temperature. In a small bowl cream the butter until light. Continue beating and gradually sift the confectioners' sugar into the butter mixture, scrape down the sides of the bowl to blend evenly. Add the cream and chocolate, beat until smooth and well incorporated.

1 1/2 ounces (1 1/2 squares) unsweetened chocolate

1/4 cup (1/2 stick) butter, softened

2 cups confectioners' sugar

2 tablespoons heavy cream

CARAMEL TOPPING

IN A small saucepan gently heat the sugar and water until the sugar has dissolved. Increase the heat and cook rapidly until the syrup is a light golden. Quickly coat the cookie and sprinkle with toasted, sliced almonds if desired.

1/2 cup sugar

1/4 cup water

White & Colored Glaze

3 cups sifted
confectioners' sugar

3 tablespoons
light corn syrup

3 tablespoons water

Food coloring

In the top of a double boiler place all the ingredients except the food coloring. Stir over simmering water until the sugar dissolves and the mixture is smooth. Remove from the heat and add food coloring a few drops at a time until the desired color is obtained. If the glaze becomes too thick add a few drops of water and beat until the desired consistency is obtained.

Chocolate Glaze & Coating

2 squares (2 ounces)
unsweetened chocolate

2 teaspoons butter

3/4 cup confectioners' sugar

Melt the chocolate and butter in the top of a double boiler over low heat. When melted sift in the confectioners' sugar a $1/4$ cup at a time. Beat the mixture, occasionally scraping down the sides of the bowl with a spatula to insure an even texture. This mixture will be very thin when warm; as it cools it hardens. Glaze cookies on wire racks over wax paper for easier clean up.

ROYAL ICING (ORNAMENTAL ICING)

MIX the egg whites and the cream of tartar beating at low speed until mixture becomes foamy, add vanilla. Gradually sift in the sugar and beat until completely dissolved. Continue beating at high speed until the mixture is light and fluffy, the beaters will leave firm peaks when lifted from the mixture. Transfer to small bowls or cups and color as desired. Keep the icing bowls covered with a damp cloth to prevent a hard shell from forming on the top of the icing. If the icing becomes too stiff, beat again at high speed with a little sugar. Thoroughly clean utensils in running water when finished to prevent "cement" from forming.

This icing dries hard and is ideal for decorations meant not to be eaten. It is edible but more useful for elaborate cookie christmas tree ornaments. This icing is usually used by bakers to form delicate flowers and elaborate decorations on cakes. It is hard and crunchy.

3 egg whites

$1/2$ teaspoon cream of tartar

$1/2$ teaspoon vanilla

1 pound confectioners' sugar

NATURAL FLAVORINGS ORANGE JUICE ICING

1 cup confectioners' sugar

Few grains salt

Orange juice

SIFT the confectioners' sugar with the salt. Add the orange juice a few drops at a time until a spreading consistency is reached. Spread on the cookies and smooth with a knife dipped in water.

VARIATIONS:
Replace the orange juice with lemonade, pink grapefruit juice, or cranberry juice.

MAPLE ICING

1/2 teaspoon butter

2 teaspoons milk

1 teaspoon maple syrup

1 1/2 cups confectioners' sugar

HEAT the milk in a saucepan milk until it is warm to the touch and pour into a mixing bowl. Melt the butter in the warm milk, add the maple syrup and combine. Gradually sift in the confectioners' sugar and beat until spreading consistency.

NATURAL FLAVORINGS PRESERVE ICING

FORCE the preserves through a sieve into a mixing bowl to remove the seeds and to produce a smoother texture. Add the lemon juice and blend well. Sift the sugar into the bowl and beat well. A small amount of cold water may be needed to produce an even spreading consistency. Decorate as desired.

VARIATIONS:
A ¼ cup of mashed fresh or frozen fruit and 2 teaspoons of sugar (or as desired) can replace the preserves, reserve some of the whole fruit and use for decoration. Use icings made with uncooked fruit soon or they will discolor.

3 tablespoons blueberry preserves

2 tablespoons lemon juice

1 cup confectioners' sugar

cold water

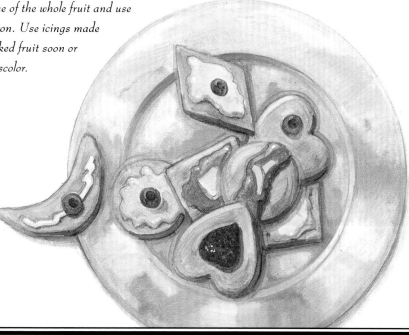

COLORING

COLORED ICING is an embellishment few pass up. The familiar boxes of liquid colors available in supermarkets are not all the choices. Alternatives include paste and powders produced in a wide range to choose from. The selection is not limited to the basics of yellow, blue, red and green. Violets, fuschias, grass greens, Christmas reds and black, to name a few have been added to the palette.

The safest method of mixing colors is to separate one recipe of white icing into a few smaller containers. This allows for more col-

ors and provides insurance against one large mistake. Cover the containers with plastic wrap to keep the icing from drying out and becoming crusty, mixing the colors or applying colored icing. Add coloring to icing or glaze a little at a time. If you are unsure of the color you want or would like to experiment, mix coloring in a small separate container, separate a small amount of icing into a clean bowl and add coloring with a tooth pick, the tip of a knife or end of a small spatula.

LIQUID food colors are easy to obtain and packaged in small plastic containers making it easy to add

colors drop by drop. They produce good color but the liquid thins out the consistency of icing. They are best used for light pastel colors, but will produce richer colors, but thinner icing.

PASTE colors produce rich, intense colors, use them carefully. Too much paste will produce dark and dreary results. A clean toothpick or the tip of a clean, small spatula should be used to remove paste from jars. Dirty

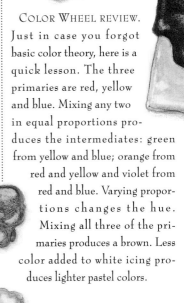

implements easily drag one color into another jar contaminating it. A bit of green left behind in a container of yellow creates a yellow-green that can never be returned to the color it originally was and renders it useless for color mixing.

POWDERED food coloring is more concentrated than paste. To use, thoroughly blend powder into a small amount of icing, then slowly add to the icing that will be used to decorate with.

Color does not need to be mixed with a icing to be used on cookies. Liquid colors can be mixed with slightly beatened egg white and applied with a small, clean artist's brush. Powdered color dissolved in a few drops of clear extract or

vodka can be applied the same way. Thin paste colors before adding to the egg and applied with a brush.

Firm doughs that will not spread during baking can be colored before baking. Be cautious, if the cookies spread during baking the painted design cracks with it.

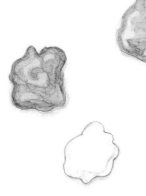

COLOR WHEEL REVIEW. Just in case you forgot basic color theory, here is a quick lesson. The three primaries are red, yellow and blue. Mixing any two in equal proportions produces the intermediates: green from yellow and blue; orange from red and yellow and violet from red and blue. Varying proportions changes the hue. Mixing all three of the primaries produces a brown. Less color added to white icing produces lighter pastel colors.

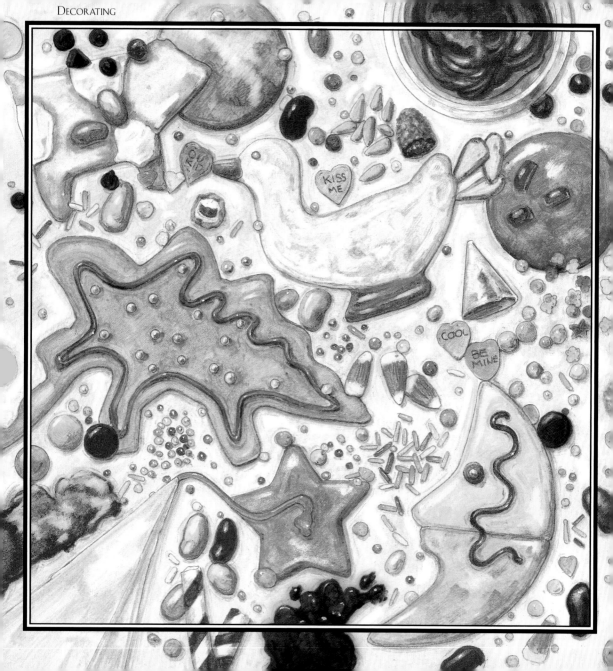

D E C O R A T I N G

FINISHING touches can be as easy as sprinkles or as dramatic as gold leaf. Icing can be simply spread with a knife or piped out with a decorating bag in graceful flourishes. Cookies can be dipped in chocolate, drizzled with glaze, topped with nuts or dotted with candy. No matter how the decorating is done each baker imprints his own style, weither it's classical, expressionist, minimalist or even primitive

Allow time to experiment with new methods and materials like marzipan and gold. Work with them to see how comfortable they are before starting a large batch of cookies. Professional bakers spend a lot of time perfecting some of their elaborate garnishes with a pastry bag and decorating tip. Don't expect to duplicate them without practice, but even the littlest squiggles of icing from a paper cone or decorating bag can add an impressive finishing touch to the humblest of cookies.

In the gallery starting on page 76 are a collection of recipes and projects combining methods previously illustrated to stir the imagination and cookie creativity.

DECORATING BAGS

Now that the icing is made and colored, applying it is the next step in the process. Smaller pastry bags than those used for meringues fitted with small tips are the most common for this type of application. There is an assortment of decorating sets available that contain a preselected assortment of tips designed for the different uses a baker might need. Decorating cookies only requires small tips, but if the desire to experiment with other tips arise manufactures like Ateco have a vast assortment to choose from. If the baker's supply in your area does not have a wide selection refer to the sources

at the back of the book for more mail order firms.

Pastry bags are manufactured in different materials for different needs, from clear plas-

Practice

tic disposables to heavy-duty construction with reinforced tips. Some reusable cloth bags have a loop or hook to hang them after they have been washed so the bags dry properly and do not crease.

Some pastry bags and most of the packaged sets come with plastic adapters to make changing the tips easier and faster. Larger bags like those used for meringue use a bigger tip that may be too big for the hole in the pastry bag. The tip used in the recipe Chocolate Rivers is one example and the bag must be cut to fit the larger tip. There are

plastic adapters for these large tips, but not easy to find. The proper method is to cut the bag. Insert the tip to be fitted into the bag, mark the outside of the bag with a pencil so that the new opening allows the tip to cover about

$1/2$ the length of the tip.

Clear polypropylene disposable bags are available to be used once and thrown away. The ends of these bags come sealed and are cut to fit the size of the tube.

Small plastic food storage bags can be used in a pinch. Simply fill the bag with icing and snip off a very small opening in one corner.

Professional bakers use paper cones rather than pastry bags for decorating. A very small opening cut in the cone allows very fine detail and if a variety of colors are needed, as many cones as needed are easily folded and filled.

PAPER CONES

PAPER CONES (also called paper cornets) require a little dexterity to make, but are well worth the effort. Use a heavy baking parchment paper cut into a triangle having 2 sides approximately 15-inch-

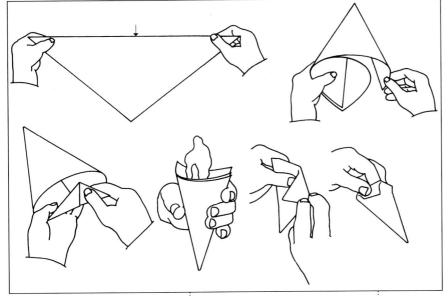

es and one approximately 20 inches or purchase the precut packages of 100. Take the tips of the long edge with your thumb and forefin-gers and roll into a cone. The point of the cone is formed in the middle of the long edge (see illustration) and the two ends in your fingertips meet the third corner. Hold the cone with thumbs in and fingers out tighten the cone to form a tight tip, at the same time make sure the seam is straight from the point to the tips of the three cor-ners. Fold the the corners inside the bag to secure it and to keep it from unrolling. The cone is now ready to be filled. Use a narrow spatula to place the icing into the cone, fill about $1/3$ full. Be careful not to soil the outside of the cone or loosen the folds. Flatten the paper above the filling, fold down one corner then the other and finally folding in the center to secure the icing. Some people like to tape the seam and the tip before adding the filling, I have not found this necessary. Cut the tip to the desired size, just remember the finer the decoration, the smaller the opening. The tips can be notched into decorating tips with a sharp knife and the icing piped out the same way as decorating bags.

FOR some people icing is glue to keep candy from falling off cookies. A small addition from the long list of choices can transform a cookie from ordinary into extraspecial. This does not mean "more is better". Candy sweetness can quickly over power the flavor and too many toppings clutter the visual affect. Toppings applied before baking should be put on after a thin wash of milk or beaten egg white is lightly applied to the formed dough with a pastry brush. Crystal sugar, candied fruit, nuts and dragees (sugar bbs), should be pressed into the dough if a wash is not used. Apply toppings to icing before it sets or a crust forms, hindering adhesion.

SOFT CANDIES applied before baking, become ugly globs in a hot oven. Candy corn, candy rocks, gum drops, gummy bears and fish, jelly beans, baby jellies, jelly fruits, licorice, marzipan fruits marshmallow miniatures are a few examples.

HARD CANDIES like cinnamon hots, confetti, conversation hearts, cut rocks, dinner mints, filled christmas candies, filled dainties, jimmies, maiden pillows, lollipops, M&Ms, non-pareils, penny candy, ribbon candy, sprinkles,

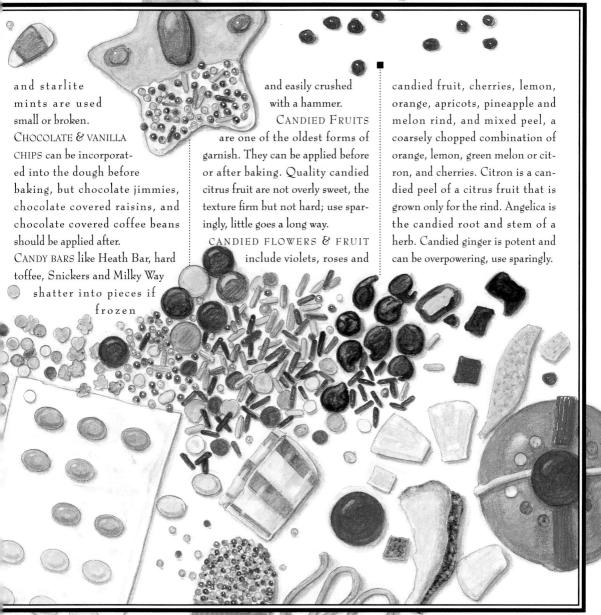

and starlite mints are used small or broken.
CHOCOLATE & VANILLA CHIPS can be incorporated into the dough before baking, but chocolate jimmies, chocolate covered raisins, and chocolate covered coffee beans should be applied after.
CANDY BARS like Heath Bar, hard toffee, Snickers and Milky Way shatter into pieces if frozen

and easily crushed with a hammer.
CANDIED FRUITS are one of the oldest forms of garnish. They can be applied before or after baking. Quality candied citrus fruit are not overly sweet, the texture firm but not hard; use sparingly, little goes a long way.
CANDIED FLOWERS & FRUIT include violets, roses and

candied fruit, cherries, lemon, orange, apricots, pineapple and melon rind, and mixed peel, a coarsely chopped combination of orange, lemon, green melon or citron, and cherries. Citron is a candied peel of a citrus fruit that is grown only for the rind. Angelica is the candied root and stem of a herb. Candied ginger is potent and can be overpowering, use sparingly.

NUTS & SEEDS

Nut meats and small seeds like almonds, anise seeds, brazil nuts, cashews, filberts, hazelnuts, macadamias, peanuts, pecans, pine nuts (piñons), pistachios, poppy seeds, pumpkin seeds, sesame seeds, shredded coconut, sunflowers and walnuts and dried fruit like currants, raisins, sultans and dates are popular as flavoring and decoration. They can be used as a garnish or added to a dough ground, chopped or sliced. Nuts and seeds contain oils that carry the flavor, but if not stored properly turn rancid or bitter. Keep nuts sealed in a cool, dark place or in the freezer until ready to use.

Some people do not like the slightly bitter outer skin of nuts and blanch to remove it.

Pecans and walnuts are never blanched

To Blanch, cover with boiling water and let stand 1 to 2 minutes. Drain, cover with cold water to stop the cooking, then drain again. Rub off the skins with fingertips or paper towels. Dry thoroughly before using or storing.

To chop nuts, use a cutting board and a sharp knife. Cut about 1/2 cup at a time into the desired size.

If large pieces or chunks are needed, walnuts, for example, can be broken by hand.

To Grate a hand-held crank type like the Mouli works well, but can only process small batches

at a time, but is easy to handle and not expensive.

To Grind use an electric food processor or blender. Process small quantities so the nuts are ground rather than crushed. Use short pulses of power and watch closely so they do not lump together or turn into an oily paste.

Break easily by putting shelled nuts in clear, plastic bags and crush them to the desired size with a rolling pin.

Flavor and texture is enhanced by roasting before using. If you need to roast them yourself, place blanched or unblanched in an ungreased,

shallow pan in a 300°F oven. Roast for $\frac{1}{2}$ to $1\frac{1}{2}$ hours until lightly browned. The time depends on the type and size of the nut, keep checking the process. Do not over cook or they will become bitter. Seal and store.

Chopped nuts, grated coconut, raisins and small seeds applied before baking should be put on after a thin wash of milk or beaten egg white is applied to formed dough lightly with a pastry brush. The cookie is gently rolled again to imbed into the dough. If a wash is not used it is important to firmly nuts press into the dough.

CITRUS RIND lemon, limes, oranges, grapefruit

tangerine; grated, slivered, chopped are used as flavorings. Fresh rind withers and dries out . Preserve rind loosely packed in granulated sugar for a few days before using as garnish.

SMALL EDIBLE FRESH FLOWERS such as lemon blossoms, orange blossoms, lime blossoms, apple blossoms, English daisies, hibiscus, honeysuckle and violets are a pretty last minute addition. Do not use sprayed flowers, remove the stamens and cut off the hard stem, secure with a small amount of fresh icing or piping gel. Storing and shipping are not recommended.

Ingredient Yields

1 pound seeded raisins equals about $2\frac{1}{2}$ cups

1 pound seedless raisins equals about 3 cups

1 pound currents equals about 3 cups

1 pound shredded or flaked coconut equals about $5\frac{1}{2}$ cups

1 pound shelled almonds, pecans, walnuts equals about 4 cups

1 pound unshelled walnuts equals about $1\frac{3}{4}$ cups nut meats

1 pound unshelled almonds equals about $1\frac{1}{4}$ cups nut meats

Marzipan

MARZIPAN is almond paste with egg white and sugar. It is used for decorations and candy and is different from almond paste. Almond paste contains almonds and sugar and is used for a variety of baking recipes.

It is available in many supermarkets and may be formed directly out of the package. If you need or would like to make your own here is a recipe.

8 ounces almond paste

1 egg white

2 cups confectioners' sugar

Food coloring

IN A small bowl break up the almond paste with a fork. Add the egg white and 1 cup sugar, and mix until well blended. Place the remaining sugar on a flat surface add almond paste and, knead until the sugar is incorporated and is smooth in consistency. About 3 minutes. Mold into desired shapes and color. Dry on wire racks and store in an air-tight container. Makes about 1 pound.

GOLD & SILVER, POWDER & LEAF

GOLD and Silver powders are non-toxic, but should not be eaten in large quantities. Mix powder in a small container with a brush and a few drops of grain alcohol (vodka, or clear flavoring extract) until smooth. If lumpy, thin with additional alcohol. Paint decorations with a brush or blend with a white icing and pipe out decorations.

Real 22 karat gold must be used. Gold is so thin it will stick to your finger tips and seemingly dissolve before your eyes. Leaf is packed between thin sheets of paper, use these separating sheets to handle the gold. Leaf will adhere to any tacky area, allow glazed cookies to dry thoroughly before gilding. Gild smooth surfaces rather than heavily frosted areas. Apply a thin coat of slightly beaten egg white or thinned piping gel with an artist's brush using a icing stencil as a guide if desired. Gently hold the leaf between two

sheets of separating paper; cut leaf with a sharp pair of scissors slightly larger than the design. Carefully remove top piece of paper covering the leaf and gently place it over the glaze. Burnish lightly with the protective paper and allow to dry completely. A protective glaze of beaten egg white may be applied when the glaze is hard.

Chocolate

Not too long ago a well respected newspaper ran an article about a group of food critics rating brands of chocolate in the same manner as they would fine wines. Chocolate lovers are very serious about their subject. Each baker must make their own selection according to taste, budget and availability.

Here are brief descriptions of the different types.

Powdered cocoa is the result of cocoa butter being filtered out of chocolate liquor.

Dutch Process is cocoa that has been treated with an alkaline solution which reduces the acidity and makes it easier to dissolve in liquids.

Unsweetened Chocolate is chocolate liquor and cocoa butter and usually sold in 8 ounce. packages of 8 one ounce cubes.

Milk chocolate is not used for baking or icing because of its low melting temperature. Do not substitute milk chocolate when the recipe calls for another type. The Chocolate Chips used in cookies are semi-sweet, not milk chocolate.

No-Melt chocolate is a compound chocolate mixed with preservatives and vegetable oil.

White chocolate contains no brown, chocolate liquor only cocoa butter, milk and sugar.

Dark German chocolate is sweetened bitter chocolate. This type is very brittle because it lacks the additional cocoa butter.

Compound or confectioners' chocolate is a term used to indicate that ingredients other chocolate liquor and cocoa butter have been used. This does not mean that the contents have been radically altered. It may mean that the manufacture has substituted another fat for cocoa butter, but it may also mean that the chocolate is artificial or synthetic and contains no ingredients from cocoa beans. Check the ingredients label if you are unsure of the contents. Some bakers prefer compounds because of the way they handle.

Couverture chocolate is also called commercial or summer coating and dipping chocolate is available in some gourmet stores in large bars and 10 pound blocks either whole or broken into 1 pound chunks. Its easy to handle, and usually has better flavor.

If a baking emergency arises the mixture equivalents on page 15 provide formulas to convert unsweetened chocolate and cocoa into bittersweet for baking.

CHOCOLATE DIPPED COOKIES

BREAK, chop, and grate the chocolate into small bits and place in the top of a double boiler over warm water or low heat. Add the shortening. Stir until almost melted. Remove from the heat and pour the mixture into a small bowl. Dip the cookie to the desired depth then hold it over the bowl, shake it and gently tap the dipped end on the side of the bowl to remove the excess. Place it on a wire rack that has waxed paper under it. Continue until the cookies are all glazed. Transfer to clean waxed paper and refrigerate until firm. Carefully separate from the wax paper, and store in plastic bags away from moisture.

Unused glaze may be poured into a glass bowl lined with foil, covered, and allowed to set in the refrigerator. When hard transfer into a plastic bag and seal. When ready to use peel the foil away, coarsely chop and slowly melt on top of a double boiler.

6 ounces semi sweet or bittersweet chocolate

1 tablespoon vegetable shortening (Crisco, not butter or margarine)

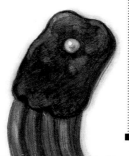

STENCILS

ICING and dusting stencils are most frequently used with confectioners' sugar and cocoa. The stencil is held over the cookie and the sugar is dusted over it. A clean pattern is achieved by holding the stencil as close as possible to the surface being dusted. Ateco (see Sources) makes a leaf stencil that is used for making leaf cookies and decorating. It looks like a broad spatula with one or two leaf designs cut out of it. It is not difficult to cut your own patterns using bond paper or a heavy paper. Simple shapes may be traced directly from ruler templates or drawn onto heavy paper and cut with a very sharp knife or razor blade. Snowflakes are cut from a sheet of bond paper. First fold the paper in half, then in half again. Note that one corner of the folder sheet has been formed at the center of the piece of paper. Using this corner as the tip fold the sides of the paper together to make a triangle, fold again to make a smaller triangle. Hold the wide end in one hand and with the other cut out small triangular notches very near the point with a sharp pair of scissors. Unfold the paper, press flat and use as a dusting pattern.

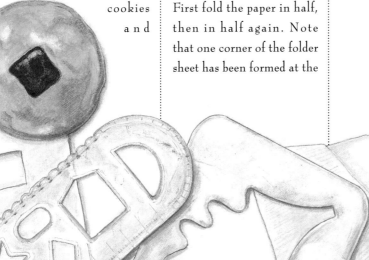

DIE-CUT PAPER

DURING the Christmas season honey cakes are cut in holiday shapes, baked, and the tops covered with decorative paper figures glued to the top with icing and removed just before eating. Images of children, flowers, animals, angels, holiday santas, gold borders, fancy alphabets and medallions are still being produced and not all of them holiday related. They have been around since the 1860s and used for Valentines, Christmas cookies, cakes and collected in scrapbooks. Antique pieces are highly collectable and can be very expensive. Do not use them as cookie decorations without sterilizing first. Use any recipe for rolled dough. Cut shapes larger than the paper figure and bake according to the directions. Allow to cool. Decorate with colored icing or glaze. Glue decorations to the cookie with beaten egg white, icing or piping gel. Allow to dry before storing. Undecorated cookies may be glazed with piping gel diluted 1 part gel to 1 part water and applied with a brush. It dries clear and hard.

THE COOKIE GALLERY

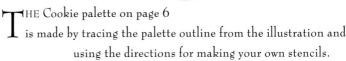

■ ....

TOAST is made by preparing the Basic Refrigerator
Cookie recipe on page 36, form the dough into a
rough rectangular cylinder and chill until firm. Form into a
bread loaf shape and chill, slice into toast and bake.
Cover with Vanilla Icing on page 53 tinted light
yellow and sprinkle with crystal
or granulated sugar.

THE Cookie palette on page 6
is made by tracing the palette outline from the illustration and
using the directions for making your own stencils.
Make the recipe for Cream Cheese Dough and roll
out to about $^1/4$ inch thick. Cut out the shape
with the stencil and the hole with the inverted
pastry tip and bake. Glaze the cooled cookies
using Colored Glaze on page 56 or a thinned Easy
Icingon page 53. Pipe out colored Cream Cheese
Icing on page 54 through a $^1/4$ inch plain
decorating tube or paper cone. Make the brush with
marzipan and paint with coloring, glue it to the
cookie with icing or piping gel.

AWARDS may be made with any of the dough recipes that can be rolled out; the Rich Basic Dough on page 18, Cream Cheese Rolled Dough on page 21, Sugar Cookie Dough on page 22, Gingerbread on page 25 or the Chocolate Wafer on page 38. Prepare the dough and roll out following the recipe instructions. Cut the top seal with a scalloped cookie cutter or trace the outline of the cookie seal on the right and make a stencil following the directions on page 32 and 33. Cut the ribbon by hand with a knife, pizza cutter or make another stencil. Bake the dough following the recipe instructions. Ice the seal and ribbon with the Colored Glaze on page 56 tint the seal yellow and the ribbon red. Glue the cookies together with icing and dot the edge of the seal with icing and place gold dragee into each. Pipe out additional decorations as desired.

PRETZELS are ropes of dough that have been twisted into shape. Use a Basic Refrigerator dough on page 32 and prepare according to the instructions. Form the dough into an even rectangle and chill until firm. Remove from the refrigerator and score the dough down the middle to divide it in half. Rotate and divide in half again; repeat two more times. The dough is now divided into 16 equal sections. Form a pretzel by rolling a rope 7 or 8 inches long with your fingers on a clean work surface. Keep the thickness of the rope as even as possible. Place the rope in a "U" shape with the ends toward you on ungreased cookie sheets. Lift the ends and twist one over the other, place the ends over the center of the "U" shape. Bake according to the directions and decorate as desired.

SNAKES are a perfect way to practice using pastry and decorating bags. The shapes are simple and forgiving. Each snake is really a squiggle and the decorations are piped with a smaller tip for a little more practice.

Fit a pastry bag with a $1/4$-inch plain, round tip and fill with the Meringue recipe on page 48 or the Chocolate Wafer recipe on page 38. Pipe out the shapes on parchment covered sheets starting with the head, pause briefly to a give the head shape, squiggle "S" shapes for the rest of the body, finish off the tail with a quick upward twist as the tip is lifted up. Bake according to the recipe directions. Allow to cool completely before decorating. Pipe the decorations with a decorating bag fitted with a small plain tip. Use dragees for eyes.

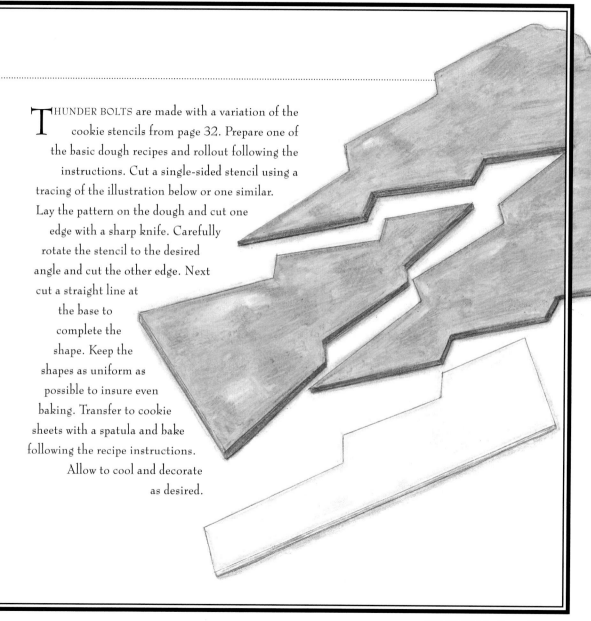

THUNDER BOLTS are made with a variation of the cookie stencils from page 32. Prepare one of the basic dough recipes and rollout following the instructions. Cut a single-sided stencil using a tracing of the illustration below or one similar. Lay the pattern on the dough and cut one edge with a sharp knife. Carefully rotate the stencil to the desired angle and cut the other edge. Next cut a straight line at the base to complete the shape. Keep the shapes as uniform as possible to insure even baking. Transfer to cookie sheets with a spatula and bake following the recipe instructions. Allow to cool and decorate as desired.

COLORED GRATED COCONUT IS made by mixing a few drops of liquid food coloring in 1 teaspoon water. Place in a sealable container with grated coconut or sugar and seal. Shake until the color is distributed evenly. Open the jar and allow the coconut to dry before using.

To color crystal or granulated sugar place 1 cup of sugar and a few drops of food coloring in a sealable jar. Seal and shake until the color is distributed evenly.

COOKIE CLOUDS are made using the stencil instructions on page 32 or any dough that may be rolled out. Trace the outline of the cloud cookie illustrations as a guide or make you own. Bake according to the recipe instruction and decorate with a blue glaze or icing. While the icing is still wet sprinkle grated coconut over the tops of the clouds. Allow to dry thoroughly before storing.

CHECKERBOARDS. Prepare the Basic Refrigerator Dough recipe on page 36. Make ½ chocolate and ½ vanilla. Shape the dough into ¼ inch thick rectangles of equal size. Straighten the edges with the flat side of a spatula. Chill until firm. Cut each piece into 2 equal parts with a sharp knife. Transfer onto a piece of wax paper by gently rolling up 1 piece around a small rolling pin and unrolling onto the wax paper. Do not stretch or thin the dough. Lightly coat top with a thin wash of beaten egg with a pastry brush. Repeat and wash with each addition layer alternating colors. Square off uneven sides with fingers or flat side of a spatula or board. Seal and chill until firm enough to cut. When firm, trim the edges perfectly straight. Cut the long side of the slab in ¼ inch pieces using a ruler if needed. Place one strip flat and brush lightly with beaten egg wash. Reverse direction of the pattern and place the next strip carefully on top of it. Brush top with egg wash and repeat until checkerboard is complete. If desired wrap in a ¹⁄₁₆ inch thick blanket of dough that has been covered with a light egg wash. Chill until firm. Slice into ¼ inch cookies, allow to warm to room temperature and bake at 350°F on parchment-lined sheets for 12 to 15 minutes.

MARBLED GLAZE is a simple classic decoration that uses two different colored glazes. Traditionally a white glaze and piped chocolate. First apply a glaze to the base of the cookie. While still wet, pipe a thin ribbon of chocolate in parallel lines over the cookie. Take the tip of a tooth pick and run it through the pattern at 90 degrees to produce a marbled affect. If you prefer use different colored glazes like red for the base and yellow for the lines.

DIFFERENT SHAPED COOKIES of can be sandwiched together with icing or preserves. Interesting shapes and combinations can be achieved by not perfectly overlapping one cookie over the other, just be certain that enough overlap exists to allow the "glue" of icing or preserves to hold the cookies together. Mixing different geometric shapes or cutting a shape within a shape adds to the variety of simple possibilities. The cookie below had a hole cut out of it using a metal pastry tip as the cutter.

P OST CARDS AND GREETINGS can be a simple as a piece of gingerbread cut in a rectangle to a large stencil of a heart for Valentines' Day decorated with die-cut paper cherubs. Decorations do not have to be elaborate, the thought that goes with them is more important.

For large shapes use a firm, rolled dough, like Gingerbread on page 22, Chocolate Cookies on page 24 or Sugar Cookies on page 25. Baking times must be watched closely, the size of the cookie changes the baking time. The larger the cookie the longer the baking. Firmer texture is easier to handle and has a better chance of surviving shipping. Allow the cookie and icing to dry thoroughly before shipping. Moist icing will crush easily and moist cookies may break.

MARBLE SWIRL

1/2 cup (1 stick) butter, softened

1/2 cup sugar

1 egg, slightly beaten

2 teaspoons vanilla

1 cup flour

2 tablespoons
ground walnuts

2 tablespoons cocoa

PREHEAT the oven to 375°F. Lightly butter the cookie sheets and set aside. Cream the butter with the sugar until smooth. Beat the egg, add the vanilla and blend thoroughly. Add the flour to the mixture and beat until well combined, scraping down the sides of the bowl occasionally to insure the ingredients are well combined. Transfer 1/2 of the batter to another bowl, mix the cocoa into one batch and the ground walnuts into the other. Blend each mixture well. Into a pastry bag or cookie press partially fill one side with one batter and force the other batter into the other side. Pipe or press onto cookie sheets. Bake until the edges are light brown and centers are just firm, about 8 to 10 minutes. Rotate cookie sheets back to front and top to bottom half way through baking. Cool on sheets 5 minutes and transfer to wire racks to cool completely. Decorate as desired.

Using this technique, other variations may include combinations of orange and lemon; almond and vanilla; or coffee and chocolate.

CHOCOLATE RIVERS

PREHEAT the oven to 375°F. In the top of a double boiler melt the chocolate and set aside to cool. Lightly butter the cookie sheets and set aside. Mix together the flour, baking powder, baking soda and salt, and set aside. Cream together the butter and sugar, add the egg and vanilla, and beat until smooth. Alternate between sifting in the dry ingredients and adding the evaporated milk and beat until well mixed.

The dough will be a little stiff. Fill a pastry bag fitted with a large, flat serrated tip and pipe onto sheets in "S" shapes by holding the bag at a 45° angle with the flat side of the tip down and the points up. These do not have to be perfect shapes, but may be adjusted with gentle finger tips. Bake 9 minutes. Rotate cookie sheets back to front and top to bottom half way through baking. Cool on sheets 3 minutes or until firm enough to transfer to wire racks to cool completely. Dip the ends first in melted semisweet chocolate then plant 1 large, gold dragee (sugar bb) into the chocolate before it sets. Place on wax paper and allow the chocolate to harden before storing.

3 ounces (3 squares) unsweetened chocolate

2 1/2 cups flour

1 teaspoon baking powder

1/4 teaspoon baking soda

1/4 teaspoon salt

1/2 cup (1 stick) butter, softened

1 1/4 cups brown sugar, hard lumps removed

1 egg, slightly beaten

2 teaspoons vanilla

1/2 cup evaporated milk

FLORENTINES

1/4 cup heavy cream

1/3 cup sugar

5 tablespoons butter

2 tablespoons flour

1/2 cup sliced almonds

1/2 cup ground almonds

1/3 cup candied orange peel, coarsely chopped

1/2 teaspoon almond extract

8 ounces semisweet chocolate

PREHEAT the oven to 350°F. Butter and flour, or cover with parchment, cookie sheets and set aside. In a saucepan over low heat combine the cream, sugar and butter, stir until the butter has melted and the ingredients are well combined. Turn the heat to medium high and bring to a boil. Remove from the heat and using a whisk add flour and ground almonds, mix well. Stir in the remaining ingredients except the chocolate. Drop by tablespoons onto the cookie sheets leaving extra space for the cookies to spread. Bake 10 to 12 minutes or until the edges are slightly brown. Rotate the sheets top to bottom and front to back halfway through baking. Allow to cool 2 minutes, then transfer to wire racks to cool completely. Melt the chocolate in the top of a double boiler and coat the bottoms of the cookies. While the chocolate is still soft run a decorating comb through it. Allow the chocolate to set before storing.

ROLLED VANILLA WAFERS

PREHEAT the oven to 425°F. Butter cookie sheets and set aside. Cream the butter and sugar until well combined. Add the egg and vanilla and beat well. Sift in the flour alternately with the half and half, beating after each addition. The batter should be very light and fluffy. Drop 2 scoops of batter (per cookie) from a tablespoon onto the baking sheet. With the back of the spoon evenly distribute the batter to about 2 1/2 inches in diameter. The batter will expand allowing only 4 cookies per sheet. Bake only 1 sheet at a time using the middle rack of the oven for 7 to 9 minutes or until the edges turn light brown. Remove from the oven and loosen from the baking sheet one at a time with a narrow, metal spatula. Quickly transfer to a clean, flat surface and roll up. Place the outside edge on the underside and allow to cool completely. Quickly repeat with the remaining cookies before they cool. The roll cookies may be placed between the rods of cooling racks to keep them from unrolling.

1/2 cup (1 stick) butter, softened

1/2 cup sugar

1 egg, slightly beaten

1 teaspoon vanilla

3/4 cup half and half

1 cup flour

ALMOND WAFERS

³/4 cup (1 ¹/2 sticks)
butter, softened

1 egg, slightly beaten

³/4 cup sugar

¹/2 cup ground almonds

2 ¹/4 cups flour

MIX together the butter, egg, sugar, and almonds, and beat well. Stir in the flour and mix well. Roll into a ball, wrap in plastic wrap or wax paper, flatten into a rectangle, seal and chill 2 to 3 hours or overnight. Preheat the oven to 375°F. On a floured surface roll the dough to about ¹/8-inch thickness and cut into desired shapes. With a spatula transfer to unbuttered cookie sheets. Bake about 10 minutes or until the edges are light brown. Rotate cookie sheets back to front and top to bottom half way through baking. Cool on sheets 5 minutes and transfer to wire racks to cool completely. Decorate as desired.

FUMI'S INEDIBLE BAKER'S DOUGH

Mix all the ingredients well. Roll out the dough and cut into desired shapes, or mold by hand into desired forms. Use a plastic straw to cut holes for hanging or stringing if desired the dough may be glued together with water to form different shapes and characters. Color with food coloring before baking. Place on an oiled pan, mold or cookie sheet. Bake at 325°F for 1 1/2 hours. For more intense colors acrylic paint may be applied after baking. Spray cookies with clear acrylic to seal. Unbaked dough may be kept in a sealed plastic bag in the refrigerator for 1 month. Just remember these cookies are inedible.

4 cups flour

1 cup salt

1 1/2 water

This dough is from my friend, Fumi. She has been using this recipe for years in the children's art classes she teaches in California. Her vast collection of treasures of dough animals, ornaments and mementos from her students are in great shape years after being presented to her.

NO BAKE NUT CRISPIES

1/4 cup (1/2 stick) butter

3 cups marshmallows

5 cups toasted rice cereal

1/2 cup chopped nuts

BUTTER a 9-inch by 13-inch baking pan and set aside. Melt the butter in a medium sized saucepan over low heat. Add the marshmallows and stir until melted and blended with the butter. Remove from the heat and while warm add the cereal and nuts, mixing well with a wooden spoon. Pour the mixture into the baking pan and quickly even out with a spatula or the back of a spoon. Refrigerate until firm. Cut into squares.

VARIATIONS:
While still warm:
add 1 cup chocolate or butterscotch chips to the mixture;
or
drizzle melted chocolate over the top;
or
sprinkle crushed hard candy over the top

GEORGINE'S COOKIES FOR A CROWD

PREHEAT the oven to 375°F. In a large mixing bowl mix the flour, baking powder and salt. Cut the butter into the flour mixture with a pastry blender or fork, add the sugar and mix until well combined. Beat in the eggs, milk and flavorings. If the dough is a little dry add a little more milk. Roll as thin as desired and cut into shapes. Bake on unbuttered sheets 8 to 10 minutes or until lightly golden. This dough is very forgiving and can be moved in and out of the refrigerator frequently and baked cookies keep in sealed tins for several months.

7 cups flour, unsifted

5 teaspoons baking powder

1 teaspoon salt

1 tablespoon butter

2 cups sugar

4 eggs, slightly beaten

1 cup milk

1 teaspoon almond extract

1 teaspoon vanilla

INDEX

EQUIPMENT & INGREDIENT SOURCES

Decorating Equipment,
  Bakeware and Supplies
Ateco
  36 Sea Cliff Avenue
  Glen Cove, NY 11542
  800 645 7170
  516 676 7100
  Fax: 516 676 7108

Broadway Panhandler
  520 Broadway
  212 966 3434
  fax 212 226 7870
  Phone Orders Only

La Cuisine
  323 Cameron Street
  Alexandria, VA 22314
  800521 1176
  703 836 4435
  Springerle and Specaulas
  Catalog available.

Wilton Bakery Division
  2240 West 75th Street
  Woodridge, IL 60517
  708 963 7100
  fax 708 963 7196
  Catalog available

Newell Group
  Mirro, WearEver, Rema &
  Foley Products
  Consumer Center
  800 527 7727

Sur La Table
  84 Pine Street
  Seattle, WA 98101
  800 240 0853
  206 448 2244
  Fax 206 448 2245
  Catalog Sales:
  800 240 0853

VillaWare
  1420 East 36th Street
  Cleveland Ohio 44114
  Electric Cookie presses

Williams Sonoma
  San Francisco, CA.
  800 541 2233

Die-cut Paper
Geno Sartori
  P.O. Box 20165
  New York, NY 10011-
  9993
  212 691 9776
  Catalog Available